Artful Moments

ADULT COLORING BOOK

MICKEY FLODIN

Lakeside Art
U.S.A.

You'll be inspired to color with this fascinating collection of expressive pen and ink drawings. Whenever your coloring mood strikes, keep it flowing with art depicting nature and the animal kingdom; such as butterflies, flowers, swans, hummingbirds, parrots, horses, turtles, and fish. You will also find graceful patterns and artistic designs to focus on and personalize. All the pages are printed on one side so you can display your art when finished. Let your imagination have freedom of expression as you peacefully enjoy each stroke of color.

Be looking for the next Coloring Book by this artist.

ISBN-13: 978-0692655085
ISBN-10: 0692655085

Printed in the United States 2016

Lakeside Art

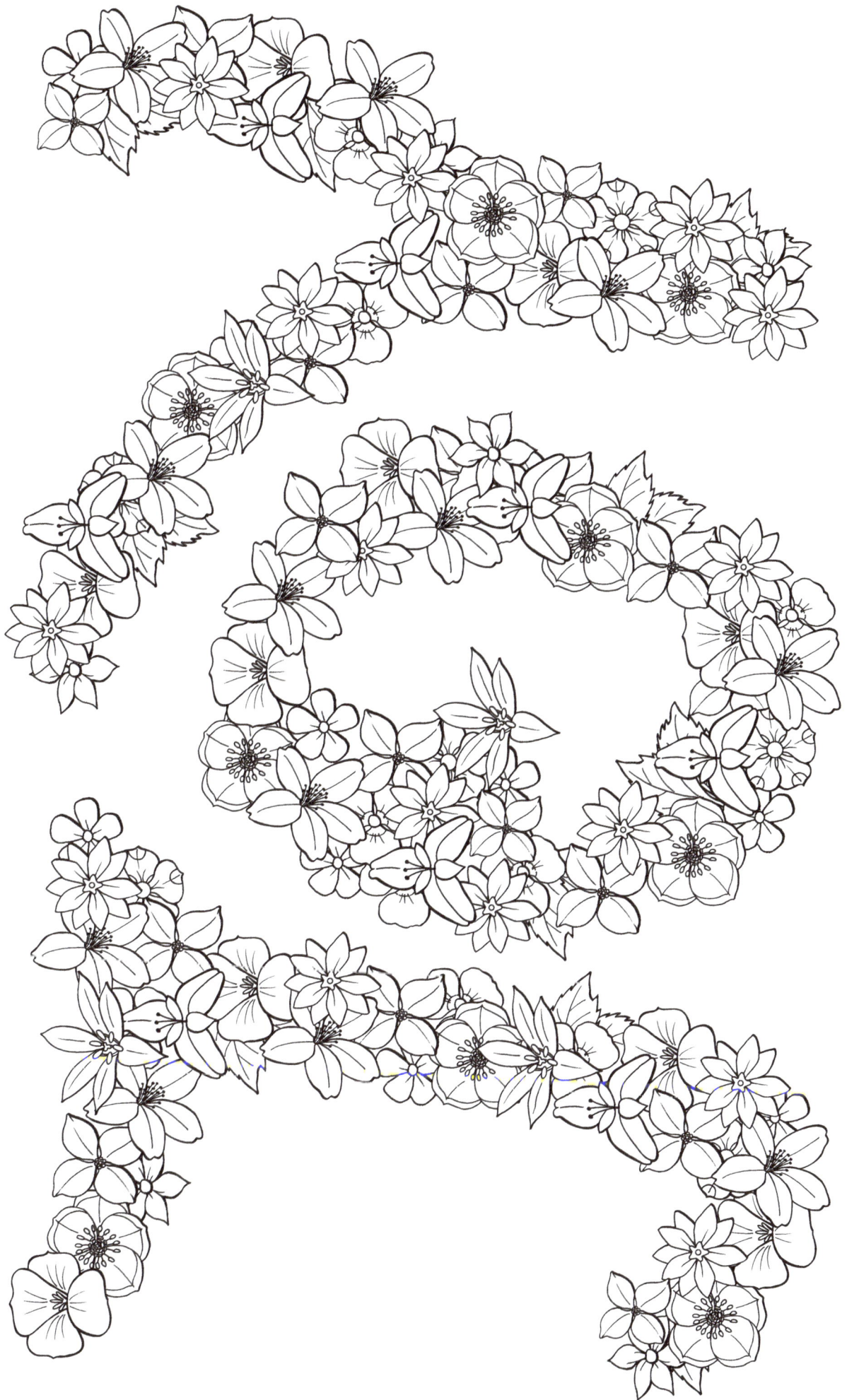

www.ingramcontent.com/pod-product-compliance
Lightning Source LLC
Chambersburg PA
CBHW080531030426
42337CB00023B/4690